HELP! MY BABY

WON'T SLEEP

The Exhausted Parent's Loving Guide to Baby Sleep Training, Developing Healthy Infant Sleep Habits and Making Sure Your Child is Quiet at Night

LEANNE PATTERSON

© **Copyright 2020** by Leanne Patterson– All rights reserved.

In no way is it legal to reproduce, duplicate, or transmit any part of this document in either electronic means or in printed format. Recording of this publication is strictly prohibited and any storage of this document is not allowed unless with written permission from the publisher.

The information provided herein is stated to be truthful and consistent, in that any liability, in terms of inattention or otherwise, by any usage or abuse of any policies, processes, or directions contained within is the solitary and utter responsibility of the recipient reader. Under no circumstances will any legal responsibility or blame be held against the author for any reparation, damages, or monetary loss due to the information herein, either directly or indirectly.

The information herein is offered for informational purposes solely, and is universal as so. The presentation of the information is without contract or any type of guarantee assurance.

Medical Disclaimer: This book does not contain any medical advice. The ideas and suggestions contained in this book are not intended as a substitute for consulting with your physician. All matters regarding you and your children's health require medical supervision.

Legal Disclaimer: all photos used in this book are licensed for commercial use or in the public domain.

ERRORS

Please contact us if you find any errors.

We have taken every effort to ensure the quality and correctness of this book. However, after going over the book draft time and again, we sometimes don't see the forest for the trees anymore.

If you notice any errors, we would really appreciate it if you could contact us directly before taking any other action. This allows us to quickly fix it.

Errors: errors@semsoli.com

REVIEWS

Reviews and feedback help improve this book and the author.

If you enjoy this book, we would greatly appreciate it if you were able to take a few moments to share your opinion and post a review online.

ENQUIRIES & FEEDBACK

For any general feedback about the book, please feel free to contact us at this email address: **contact@semsoli.com**

Dedication

I dedicate this book to all the superhero moms and dads out there who, exhausted as they may be, get up at 4am, night after night, to check on their baby once more.

<u>You are amazing</u>, and you're doing **a great job**.

Never doubt that!

Table of Contents

INTRODUCTION..**11**

CHAPTER 1: IS THERE SOMETHING WRONG? **17**

    Why Does My Baby Cry Then?

    Rule Out The Obvious

    Next Check If There May Be A Medical Reason

    Teething

    Separation Anxiety

    Sniffles and Fevers

    Gas And Colic

    Ear Infections

    Allergies And Asthma

CHAPTER 2: GETTING THE CRYING TO STOP...**31**

    Try Movement

    Rocking Baby

    Let Baby Be A Swinger

    Let Baby Help With The Laundry

Getting Your Baby Comfortable

Make It A Wrap

Raise The Roof

Try Using Touch

Baby Massage

Distraction

CHAPTER 3: NATURAL REMEDIES TO HELP YOUR BABY SLEEP AT NIGHT 45

Herbal Teas

Essential Oils

Three Ways To Use Essential Oils

Natural "Remedies" You Don't Want To Try

CHAPTER 4: THE CRY IT OUT APPROACH 55

Cry It Out Approach

An Alternative

Which Should I Choose?

CHAPTER 5: MAKING YOUR BABY'S SLEEPING ENVIRONMENT A SAFE PLACE 61

Sudden Infant Death Syndrome (SIDS)

Check The Crib For Comfort And Safety

CHAPTER 6: HOW DOES YOUR BABY SLEEP?..67
- Baby Is Still Developing
- When Will My Baby Sleep Through The Night?

CHAPTER 7: SETTING UP A DAYTIME ROUTINE 71
- Observe Your Baby
- Some Helpful Tricks
- Come Up With A Plan Of Action
- Daytime Should Also Have A Routine
- Monitor The Number Of Feeds During The Day
- Monitor What They Eat
- Daytime Naps

CHAPTER 8: YOUR NIGHTTIME ROUTINE........83
- Two Hours Before Bedtime
- An Hour Before Bedtime
- When Is A Good Bedtime?

FINAL WORDS 87

RESOURCES 89
- Websites
- Books
- For Fun

DID YOU LIKE THIS BOOK?	91
NOTES	92

INTRODUCTION

Does your home turn into a battleground each night when it is time for your baby to go to sleep?

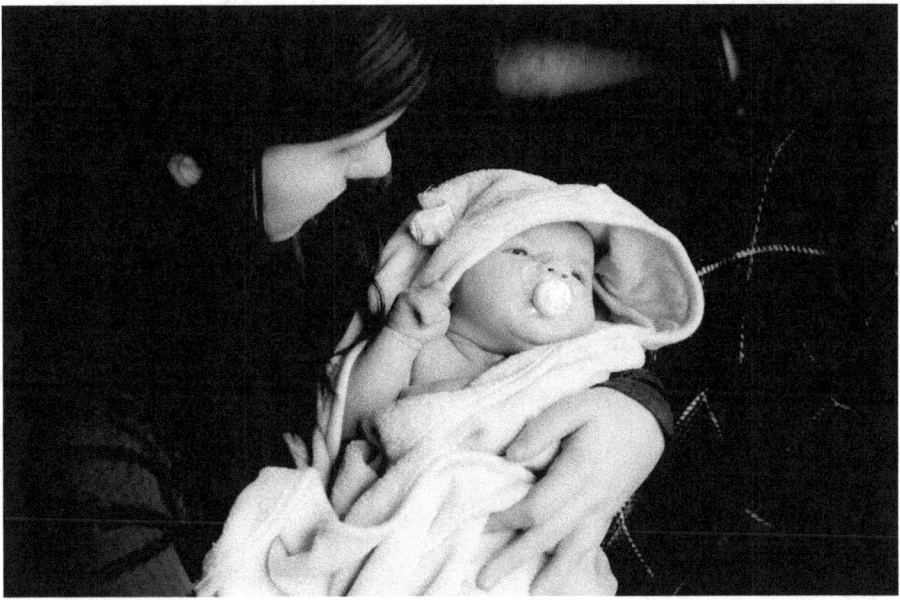

Or does your baby fall asleep in your arms peacefully, only to wake up crying 2 hours later at a volume that would make Guns N' Roses' sound technician jealous?

If you are reading it as a bleary-eyed parent of a newborn, desperate to get some sleep, welcome to the club. Everyone who has had kids has been there. Anyone who tells you any different is either lying or had someone else to take care of their baby.

So, welcome aboard the midnight express. I can't promise that it won't be a bumpy ride, but I can guarantee that by reading this book you are taking your first steps to getting back to something resembling a regular sleep schedule.

Being a new parent is exhausting – you have read all the baby books but, unfortunately, your baby hasn't. If you get as exhausted as I was at one stage, you start using that information to reason with your baby. I once caught myself trying to have a rational conversation with a screaming six-month-old. Apparently, he didn't care that the baby book said he had to have a set routine.

So yes, I have been there. I have been right out there at my wit's end. I have tried begging, pleading, and I'm not proud to admit, bribing my child to go to bed. I have caught myself yelling back, "What do you want?" and feeling like an absolute failure because I didn't even know what my baby needed.

The baby books tell you how things ought to go. They make it all sound so easy. Do you know what I learned, though? It's not as simple as all that. Each kid is different and what worked for one won't necessarily work for the rest.

Know what else? **It doesn't make you a bad parent**. Babies aren't rational, considerate beings – they can be little angels, but they can also be little devils. There will be times when you can't believe you can love something so much, and times when you just want to run away.

Don't stress about it – that's parenting for you. You are here because you need help. And help you I will. In this book, I am going to teach you what to do when your kid doesn't stop crying. You will learn what you can do straight away to get some peace and quiet. (Without running off to join the circus.)

But we're not going to stop there. We are going to look at how you can prevent future meltdowns and get to a point where your child goes to bed and falls asleep with minimal fuss and minimal effort.

Here is what we're going to cover:

- **Chapter One: Is There Something Wrong?** Before diving into possible solutions, you will first need to make sure nothing is physically wrong with your precious one. If your baby is ill, drinking tea won't help. Your baby needs a medical examination.
- **Chapter Two: Getting The Crying To Stop**. After you have ruled out any illness, how do you get your baby to stop crying? This chapter contains many recommendations, such as different ways in which you can rock your baby and make it feel comfortable.
- **Chapter Three: Natural Remedies To Help Your Baby Sleep At Night**. In addition to what you learned in Chapter Two, in this next chapter you will learn how you can use natural remedies such as herbal teas and essential oils to put baby to sleep.
- **Chapter Four: The Cry It Out Approach**. Here you will not only learn the Cry It Out approach, but also an alternative approach. Ultimately, you have to do your own experiment and see which one works best for both you and your baby.

- **Chapter Five: Making Your Baby's Sleeping Environment a Safe Place**. Another big one is making sure your baby feels safe. It spent 9 months in a very safe environment that never changed. Now it's falling asleep in a brightly lit living room, and waking up the next moment in a dark bedroom. Making sure your baby's bedroom is safe and feels comfortable to baby can make a big difference.
- **Chapter Six: How Does Your Baby Sleep?** Your baby is still developing, and doesn't share your sleeping cycle. Realizing this, and understanding that this will change with time, can reduce the stress you experience.
- **Chapter Seven: Setting Up A Daytime Routine**. In this chapter you will learn how you can set up a daytime routine that will help baby to fall asleep faster in the evening, and sleep for longer.
- **Chapter Eight: Your Nighttime Routine.** Finally, we will go over what would be a good nighttime routine for you that is conducive to your baby falling and staying asleep.

Be prepared; this is real life, not a Disney movie. You're going to have to pull up your sleeves and learn a few tricks but, I promise, it will be worth it in the end.

Ready. Steady. Let's go!

CHAPTER 1: IS THERE SOMETHING WRONG?

"There was never a child so lovely but his mother was glad to get him to sleep." **Ralph Waldo Emerson**

In this chapter, you will learn what to check for to make sure nothing is physically wrong with your baby.

Many new parents blame themselves if they cannot get their child to stop crying. I want to stop you right here. Lose the guilt trip and relax. It's normal for a baby to cry and you are not a bad parent for not knowing why they are crying.

What you need to remember is that your baby can pick up vibes from you very quickly. So, if you are all tense about the crying, they are also going to be more agitated as a result. The calmer you are, the more relaxed baby will be.

It is easy to give advice, sitting here in my lovely quiet office without a baby squalling in my ears, but it is valid advice nonetheless. Take a deep breath and calm down. Give yourself a break and then get back into the ring and try again.

Why Does My Baby Cry Then?

Sometimes he wakes up and is hungry or thirsty. Sometimes he just wants his parents. We all get lonely at times. He might be confused – when he went to sleep, things looked very different. In the blink of an eye, his entire world has changed.

Think how you would feel if you fell asleep in your bed at night and woke up the next day in an entirely different room, and that place was dark and cold. You'd be confused, wondering where you were and how you got there. You might start crying yourself if that happened to you.

Now that you understand a little more about the baby psyche, let's see what steps you need to take.

Rule Out The Obvious

Begin by ruling out the obvious:

- ☐ Check the diaper and change it if necessary
- ☐ Check if the baby is hungry
- ☐ Is he too hot, or too cold?
- ☐ Has he hurt himself?
- ☐ Are his clothes too tight or restrictive for him?

Next Check If There May Be A Medical Reason

You should have an infant thermometer to check baby's temperature. Is it higher than usual? Do they feel feverish? Do they seem cold and clammy? When baby's temperature is high, get them to the pediatrician or emergency room as fast as possible. If you are in doubt, get them to the doctor.

Teething

This will often prevent your baby falling asleep. Think about when you last had a cavity and the agony you had to go through before it got sorted out. Now imagine that kind of pain with all your teeth.

Teething is sore, and your baby is not going to be able to verbalize what the problem is. Teething can start in babies from about three months onwards, so look out for:

- ☐ Trouble sleeping
- ☐ Being fussy
- ☐ Drooling more than the dog
- ☐ A runny nose
- ☐ Biting more than normal
- ☐ A rash on the lower half of the face

- Cheeks that are rosy all the time
- Not wanting to eat or drink
- Trying to suck more often.
- Gums that look inflamed

If teething is the issue, there are a few things that you can do to help ease the pain. You can buy teething rings that can be kept in the refrigerator. The baby sucks on these, and the cool temperature helps to numb the gums.

Alternatively, you can give them a cold, damp washcloth to suck on. (But do make sure that you are there to watch them if you are doing this, so they don't choke on it.)

You can make up a little bottle of cream as described in Chapter Three, containing Lavender oil and chamomile oil, and apply it to the cheeks, not the inside of the mouth. It will offer relief for the pain and help heal the rash if there is one. You can lightly massage the gums and apply an O.T.C. teething gel if nothing else works.

Separation Anxiety

Babies like routine. Changes in routine can upset them. Like when mom must go back to work, or they have to start going to kindergarten. This can have an unsettling effect on their nighttime routine.

At this early age, they still don't have a real concept of how long the day is. What just a few hours are for you can seem like a lifetime for them.

The way to counteract this is to be particularly loving to them when you are at home. When you drop the baby off, tell them you are leaving and leave with a smile on your face. You want them to think that your leaving is a good thing.

Give them something to remind them of you while they are away. Maybe it could be a toy that smells like mommy – like a little lovey. Something that they can snuggle when they cannot get access to mommy or daddy.

Get them used to not being able to see you every now and again in the build-up to the main event. Leave them alone for a minute or two every now and again. Say, "I'm just going out quickly" and leave the room, so they get used to short absences.

Sniffles and Fevers

If your baby has a mild cold, and a low fever, you can help him feel better by letting him rest as much as possible.

Make sure that he gets a lot of liquids in so that he doesn't get dehydrated. If your baby is old enough to drink tea, find him some Chamomile Tea or Red Bush Tea and give him that. It will help replenish some of the minerals that he is losing. Make sure it's not too hot! Lukewarm is best.

If the child is old enough, you could let them suck some ice chips or a popsicle. If they are still very young, you might find that bathing them in tepid water or changing their clothes when they are soaked is a good idea.

Do help clear the mucus out of their nose and put a humidifier in the room so that their airways don't dry out. And finally, the main ingredient is lots of T.L.C. (Tender Loving Care) from you and your partner.

Gas And Colic

Babies all get gas, as you will know if you have ever tried to burp them. For me, it's incredible how much air they can swallow.

Gas causes them pain, and so all you may need to do is to burp baby gently. This could be done by patting them on the back and bottom, massaging their backs or gently massaging their tums. You could also try to move their legs in a circular motion (as if they were riding a bike) to push out the gas.

Colic is a more difficult one. We are not precisely sure what the cause of colic is, but there are those that believe that it might be because of too much sensory stimulation.

Your baby may have colic if:

- They regularly cry their hearts out, especially in the afternoon or later.
- They cry non-stop for an hour or more.
- They are up to the age of four months old.
- They have no other health issues and are happy to play at various times.

Treating colic is not so easy but here are some things that you can try:

- Let baby feed as often as they need to to keep them calm. Preventing the meltdown in the first place is the best solution.
- If you are breastfeeding, stay away from foods that cause an increase of gas in the system and avoid overstimulating compounds such as caffeine.
- If you are using formula, try a different brand, or try institute smaller meals at a more frequent interval.
- Change the type of nipple on the bottle that you are using to one that does not allow a lot of air in.
- Keep baby upright when you are feeding them.
- Feed him in a relaxed, calm place.
- Burp your baby more often.
- Carry them closer to you during this time – a baby sling is a great baby "handsfree" kit.
- Soak a washcloth in tepid water and place over baby's tummy or let them have a nice little bath.

Colic should go away on its own when your baby is four months old so, if all else fails, there is an end in sight. If you can, make some plans to have a break occasionally. Let your partner look after the baby when they are grumpy so that you can take some time off. Do the same for them. This will help you stay sane.

See your doctor about it if:

- Your baby is vomiting as well.
- It goes on past four months.
- Your baby won't let you pick them up.
- Your baby is sore.
- Your baby is not gaining weight as they should.
- They have long crying spells more than once a day.
- Their bowel movements are irregular or have changed.

Ear Infections

This is another one that can be difficult to figure out because it's not immediately clear.

Symptoms might be:

- [ ] A fever
- [ ] An "I am sore" cry
- [ ] Fussiness
- [ ] Pulling at the ear
- [ ] Not letting you near the ear
- [ ] A runny nose but no other cold symptoms
- [ ] Discharge from the ear
- [ ] Not wanting to eat
- [ ] An unpleasant smell from the ear
- [ ] Baby not being able to hear you as well as usual

This is one area where you want to whisk them off to the doctor. He (or she) will be able to say for sure what the problem is and what it is not. Ears are a sensitive issue as a lot can go wrong. Don't take a chance here.

The doctor may give you something to help with the pain and with the infection. Don't use any other drops or things like that.

You can:

- [ ] Raise the crib slightly so that the baby's head is a little higher than the rest of him.

- You can soak a washcloth in warm water, wring it out and apply over the ear to soothe it.
- Keep water out of the ear.
- Make sure baby gets enough to drink.
- You can make a Lavender and Chamomile cream, as described in Chapter Three, and apply it to the OUTSIDE of the ear. Work it in gently from the inner edge of the ear, down the side of the face and past the jawline because the tube extends further down. Dab a bit directly behind the earlobe as well.

Allergies And Asthma

Babies that battle to breathe, whether because of a cold, allergy or asthma, will have trouble staying asleep.

Your child may have asthma or an allergy if they:

- Have a runny nose
- Have the sniffles or sneeze a lot
- Cough a lot
- Always seem to have a blocked nose
- Have itchy eyes, nose, and ears
- Have watery eyes

- ☐ Complain of a sore throat
- ☐ Battle to breathe
- ☐ Have breakouts
- ☐ Have diarrhea

If you suspect your child has asthma or allergies, you must take them to the doctor for a proper diagnosis.

Before we move, let's do a quick recap of this chapter. You have learned:

- ☐ The obvious things to rule out when your baby is crying
- ☐ How to tell if they are teething
- ☐ How to tell that they have separation anxiety
- ☐ How to tell if it is a cold or flu
- ☐ How to tell if it is gas or colic
- ☐ How to tell if it is an ear infection
- ☐ How to tell if it is allergies or asthma
- ☐ What you can do if it is one of the conditions listed above

In the next chapter, you will learn ways to ease your baby's crying.

CHAPTER 2: GETTING THE CRYING TO STOP

"Sleep, baby, sleep. Thy father's watching the sheep. Thy mother's shaking the dreamland tree, and down drops a little dream for thee."
Elizabeth Prentiss

In this chapter, you will learn how to get the crying to stop.

This and Chapter Three are your first aid kit for when something goes wrong. For now, all we are doing is to get the wailing to stop; we'll talk about setting up a routine in a later chapter.

Your baby has been crying all night, you've checked everything. Baby's diaper is clean; he's not hungry. You've begged, you've cried yourself, and there is nothing else you can think of to do. You desperately want the baby to sleep or, at the very least, stop crying.

Try Movement

You've been there before. As a last resort, you put the baby in the car seat and drive around at three in the morning. Then, blissful silence as baby falls asleep. The reason that this works is that baby is used to being in motion about all the time.

When they are in the womb, they move around a lot and so does their mother. Movement can remind them of being in the womb and thus make them feel comfier.

You don't, however, need to drive around at three in the morning like a zombie. Try the following tricks first.

Rocking Baby

A rocking chair is essential in any nursery, especially if you have a baby on the fussy side. The motion of the chair is soothing for baby, and it helps support mom and dad as well. (Babies, though small, can seem heavy when you are tired.) Use gentle movements.

Alternatively, rock them in your arms by making small, rhythmic movements.

Let Baby Be A Swinger

Do you have a swing? A swing that you can buckle baby into is another effective way of rocking them to sleep. This is especially great if you are tired because you can get a motorized version that does all the work for you.

Let Baby Help With The Laundry

This is good for two reasons:

- It helps you tick one chore off your list, and
- It could soothe the baby.

Place your baby in their car seat and buckle them in. Load up your washing and set the timer. Put the seat onto the machine.

You will have to hold it in place, so you'll have to stay there, but this should help baby nod off. Just a word of caution here, use the car seat, or something similar; something that supports that baby's whole body, neck, and head. You don't want to use a bassinette with no neck support because then they could bounce around in it and hurt themselves.

Also, don't take your eyes off them for a second. If you desperately need to go into another room, either switch off the machine or take the baby seat off and place it on the floor.

The technique will work with your washer and dryer.

Getting Your Baby Comfortable

The key to getting baby off to sleep and getting them to sleep for longer is in keeping them comfortable. Try some of the following to get them sleepier:

- **Nesting**: This is where you cocoon the baby in their car seat or your arms, etc. Do keep an eye on your infant while doing this though, and only do this if they can hold their heads upright. Let them sleep flat out from time to time so that they get used to sleeping in both positions.
- **Smells**: Babies can be hypersensitive when it comes to odor. In nature, that is how animals recognize their own kind. Take advantage of this fact by using baby's favorite small cuddly toy. Keep it close to your body for a little while and then put it into the crib with the baby so that they have the scent of the familiar when they wake up. It must be something that is not large enough to smother them and not small enough to fit in their mouths.
- **Temperature**: Warm the crib a little before baby climbs in. It should be body temperature, or they might get woken up by the cold crib mattress. You could also use winter sheeting as an alternative as this doesn't get quite as cold.
- **Big Meal**: A big meal can have the same soporific effect on a baby as it does on an adult. Make sure that your baby has their full meal before they go to sleep or they will wake up very quickly for another feeding.

Make It A Wrap

- **Swaddling**: This is a trick that may help your baby to feel more secure. Newborns are used to being in a very confined environment, and so swaddling might help replicate that. Keep it for nighttime use to help them associate it with sleep. There are a few contraindications when it comes to swaddling, though. Make sure that you wrap them in a light blanket that is made of natural fibers to improve breathability. Keep it for when the room is cool and stop doing it when the baby starts moving around.
- **Snuggly Bunny**: This is good for young babies especially. Remove baby's clothes and then let them nestle against your naked skin. Cover with a nice warm blanket. This helps them feel more secure and snuggled.
- **Sling it**: No, I <u>don't</u> mean slinging your baby. Although after the millionth hour of crying that starts to become tempting...I suggest using a sling that straps the baby to you. This can remind the baby of the confinement of the womb and give you the freedom to move around a bit as well.

Raise The Roof

Remember the good old days when you could still party up a storm? Now, if someone so much as drops a pin when the baby is sleeping, you are ready to kill them. That's mistake number one.

The womb is not some serene little bubble that completely shuts out the noise. The baby can hear some sounds from outside, your heart beating and even the blood rushing through your veins.

Now, while you don't want to play party tracks at full volume, a little bit of noise can help soothe your baby.

- **White Noise Machine**: This can be one of your best friends. It helps to drown out the sounds of the house and mute them. Also, it gives the baby some background noise to calm him down.
- **Fans Help**: If you have a fan in the room, the noise might help calm baby down. Just make sure that the fan is not blowing directly on him.
- **Shush Baby**: Hold baby close and say, "Shush" softly to him. This replicates the noise that they might have heard in the womb.

- **Music**: Is there music that calms your child down? Try playing it softly. It could be classics, it could be something with a rhythmic beat, or it might even be heavy metal. Watch baby to see what music they enjoy and find calming.
- **Vacuum**: This is another way to get chores ticked off the list and earn some clever parent points at the same time. The sound of the vacuum and the motion of you doing the vacuuming could help baby nod off.
- **Heartbeat**: In the womb, the baby hears your heartbeat as a steady and regular rhythm. If the baby is fussy, try holding him close to your chest so that he can listen to your heartbeat. You can also find recordings of heartbeats online and play these to the baby instead of music.
- **Read**: Get out baby's favorite book and read to him. The combination of your voice and the story that they love will often soothe them. Get used to the fact that you are going to end up reading the same book every night for the next couple of years.
- **Sing to them**: Your baby loves your voice. It doesn't matter that you cannot carry a tune or if you were kicked out of choir practice. Your singing is soothing for your child anyway.

- **Talk in a soft tone**: It doesn't matter what you say, just speak softly and lovingly to them.

Try Using Touch

Touch can be very soothing for a small child. Start by rubbing their back in long, slow strokes. Repeat with their arms and legs. This can have a very soothing effect.

Give your baby the odd cuddle, or massage throughout the day, like when you change his diaper or feed him.

If nothing else is working, try taking the baby to the bathroom and run a warm bath. The sound of the water is soothing, and so is the bath itself. Follow bath time with a massage for a completely relaxed baby.

Baby Massage

Use a gentle touch and baby oil, nice-smelling lotion or cream you have made yourself. Dry baby off after his bath and put his diaper on for him. Lay him out on a surface that you can reach easily, and that is comfortable for him. The sofa or your lap is ideal.

Throughout the massage, watch your baby's reactions. Is it relaxing him or making him even fussier? If the latter, stop and try something else. A full body massage starts at the head and works all the way down to the soles of the feet. Watch which parts baby likes best, and you can concentrate on those if you are short of time in the future.

Start by stroking his face with your hands, in a gentle cupping motion. Work your way down the face. Gently massage the temples using one finger on each and a circular motion, move outward until you get to the hinge of baby's jaw.

Carry on outwards like this and work your way from behind each ear until you have covered the whole scalp. (Just avoid the fontanelle, the soft spot in the skull.)

You can now move onto stroking the arms. Pull gently at the arms as if you were milking a cow. When you get to the hands, stroke the palms using your thumbs and very gently squeeze each finger before pulling it a little.

Move down to the chest, and stroke downwards using firm strokes until you reach the abdomen, use short, light strokes, changing position often.

Move on to the legs and, again, wrap your hand around the thigh. Gently pull downwards and stroke the thigh. Work your way down to baby's ankle and back up again to the hip.

Move on to baby's feet and repeat the process you used for the hands.

Turn baby over and massage the back and bottom with firm downward strokes. With just two fingers of each hand, rub the muscles next to the spine in a circular motion from the neck down to the bottom.

Massage his neck and shoulders gently and then finish off with a final few strokes on the back of his legs.

Distraction

This, as I learned quite by accident, can be very effective. One day I was looking after my little one, and I could not get him to stop crying. I tried everything I could think of. Eventually, I cried loudly as well. (I don't recommend this – please don't judge, I was at the end of my rope.)

It distracted him long enough to stop him crying and so a new technique was learned. In future, I tried distractions that were a little more humane, like giving him something shiny to play with, or a new toy, or getting him to play with our dog.

The key is that he got so engrossed, that he forgot to be in a bad mood.

Let's recap this chapter. You have learned different ways to stop baby's crying:

- ☐ Movement can soothe babies.
- ☐ Some noises can be soothing.
- ☐ Sometimes baby just wants to be close to you.
- ☐ The value of touch cannot be overestimated.
- ☐ Your baby loves the sound of your voice.
- ☐ Massage is beneficial for babies.
- ☐ If all else fails, distraction might work.

In the next chapter, you will learn about natural remedies that are safe for use with babies and that might help calm them down.

CHAPTER 3: NATURAL REMEDIES TO HELP YOUR BABY SLEEP AT NIGHT

"Having my baby fall asleep in my arms takes away all of my worries and stresses. A sense of complete and total peace comes over me." **Maria Jose Ovalle**

In this chapter, you will learn about natural remedies that will help your baby sleep at night.

I would like to preface this by saying that even natural remedies can have side effects so use them wisely. While the following remedies are quite safe, it is *essential* that you speak to your pediatrician before applying any of them.

When using any natural remedies, it is important to remember that your baby should not receive the same dose that you as an adult would take.

Herbal Teas

Herbal teas are remedies that have been used throughout the centuries for fussy babies who won't stop crying. The main advantage of herbal teas is that they have no caffeine and can have very soothing properties.

he teas mentioned below are safe and natural, but that doesn't mean that you can go nuts with them! Before starting with any of the teas, speak to your pediatrician. You should only start your baby out with the tea when they are six months or older. Also, make sure the tea isn't too hot. Lukewarm is best.

Make a weak tea with any of the herbs listed below and see if the baby will drink it unsweetened. If they won't, try adding a little bit of sugar. Honey is another sweetening alternative but only if your child is over a year old. This is critical advice – children under the age of a year cannot fight the botulism-causing spores that may be found in honey. If in doubt, skip it completely.

Herbal teas are better if given black, but if that is not working, you can also add a little milk to make them a little more palatable. It is best to use organic sources for the teas that your little one will be drinking. Some of the herbs, like Lemon Balm, can easily be grown at home so that might be a more practical option for you.

I recommend trying one of the following herbal teas:

- **Chamomile Tea**: This is a tried and tested remedy that has been used in Europe for ages. Make up a bottle of chamomile tea and let baby sip it about half an hour before bedtime to help calm them down. This promotes a deeper sleep and is very soothing. It is also a good anti-spasmodic and can soothe an upset tummy.

- **Rooibos Tea (Red Bush Tea):** This has its origins in South Africa. This has a more palatable flavor and similar calmative properties to the Chamomile tea. It makes a great iced tea for those sweltering summer days. Mix Chamomile and Rooibos together for a calming tea with a pleasant taste.
- **Lemon Balm (Melissa):** If you have a fussy baby that is over-tired and won't sleep, Lemon Balm is an excellent soother for both of you. Make yourself a cup when making baby's. A half-teaspoon of the fresh herb in a cup of boiling water is plenty.
- **Fennel Seed or Caraway Seed Tea:** These are excellent for soothing an upset tummy and clearing out the wind. Boil a teaspoon of the seeds in four cups of water for around ten minutes. Strain and allow to cool before giving it to the baby.

Essential Oils

Essential oils can be a very powerful helpmate when it comes to soothing your child. That said, they are extremely concentrated and, if misused, can harm the baby.

Here are the rules to follow when it comes to essential oils:

- Do not use any form of essential oils with your child before they are three months old.
- NEVER let them take the oils internally.
- NEVER apply the oils neat. (Lavender is the exception, but I would still dilute it before using it on baby's skin.)
- From three months onwards, you may use Lavender oil, Mandarin oil, or Chamomile oil. Don't use any others until they get older.
- The oils can be used in a diffuser with a drop or two of the oil in at most, for about half an hour, to calm baby or prepare him for sleep. Do NOT leave the diffuser on longer than that.
- They can only be used on the skin of your baby if highly diluted. That means no more than a 1% concentration. Mix them in with a plain aqueous cream or baby oil. Alternatively, dissolve a drop in half a cup of mix and use it in baby's bath. If used directly on the skin they can cause irritation and burns.
- From the age of about two years on, you can start using Eucalyptus oil to help clear up baby's stuffy nose and help them sleep more soundly.

- The plant compounds within the oils can build up to toxic levels if the oils are used in too high concentration, or over too long a period. So, switch it up from time to time. If you are using Lavender this week to help baby sleep, switch over to Chamomile next week or take a break with the oils altogether.
- Finally, if your kids are little climbing monkeys, lock the oils away where they cannot be found.

Personal story: *My two-year-old nephew got hold of my batch of essential oils in the few minutes it took me to go from the bedroom to answer the door. I was gone for two or three minutes, and he'd climbed up the cupboard, pulled out a bottle and splashed the contents liberally on his cheeks. If this does happen to you, dampen a cloth with milk and apply it to the area. Milk and NOT water because the oils dissolve in the milk. Use the cloth to mop it up. Rinse off again with clean, warm water and apply plain aqueous cream liberally. In my case, I was lucky because I got there as he was splashing the oils on. In the end, his skin was just a little red from experience, but it could have been a lot worse.*

Here are some oils that you might want to consider:

- **Lavender**: This is a good, all-purpose oil that can be used to calm baby from the age of three months onwards. Lavender oil is a healer that can also be used for cuts, abrasions, mild burns, and bruises and to relieve pain. It is very soothing and can be effectively used in a diffuser to promote calmness, and help baby sleep soundly. Lavender mixes well with Chamomile, either in a diffuser or in an aqueous cream, to help soothe the little one's nerves. In an aqueous base, it is excellent for diaper rash.
- **Chamomile**: This is an incredibly calming oil for your little one and one of nature's best analgesics. It can be used from three months onward. If the baby is teething, dilute the oil into some aqueous cream and rub onto the cheeks and the jaw area to help baby cope with teething pains. Adding Lavender can also boost this effect. If your baby is suffering from an upset tummy or a lot of wind, massage a mixture of Lavender and Chamomile oil gently into their belly.
- **Mandarin**: This is gentle enough to be used on baby from three months on. It helps to calm and soothe and can be a valuable alternative to Lavender or Chamomile if baby does not like the smell of those.

- **Eucalyptus**: This is only safe to use from two years on and should be used in a weak concentration. You can mix it with Lavender to boost its efficacy. It is excellent for clearing up snotty noses and can be diffused into the room to help clear congestion or to kill germs if others in the house are ill. It is also useful for relaxing tight and sore muscles so can be useful if the baby has been crying up a storm.

Three Ways To Use Essential Oils

There are three ways in which I recommend you use essential oils:

- **Diffuse the oils** – one or two at a time.
- **In a rub** – Mix with aqueous cream, baby oil or Sweet Almond oil. Use to gently massage baby as we spoke about in the earlier chapter.
- **In a tub** – Drop two drops or so into a half a cup of milk to disperse the oils. Draw the bath and, when it is at the right temperature, add the milk.

This simple rhyme will help you remember them:

In a rub, in a tub but never, ever in my grub.

In some mist or some steam, all the better to help me dream.

Natural "Remedies" You Don't Want To Try

I remember at my twenty-first birthday when my mother toasted me and told us all about the time that she followed some old-fashioned advice that went wrong. When I was a baby, she had been told that a teaspoon of whiskey would send me straight off to sleep.

Apparently, it did not – it made me even more hyperactive. The moral of the story is that when your child is not sleeping, and you are dead tired, you are about ready to try anything. In this case, no harm was done to me, but it could have gone a lot worse.

If you get what you think is dodgy advice, speak to your pediatrician first before trying it. As tired as you are, drugging or intoxicating your child is never going to be the right option for you to try. Look for a different way.

All the remedies that we have spoken about in this book are natural and safe to use, and at least one of them should work. There are, however, going to be times when the baby is just not going to want to sleep. As adults, we just must accept that.

In this chapter, we discussed natural remedies to help your baby sleep at night. Let's recap what you have learned:

- There are natural remedies that can be as effective as medication.
- All natural remedies should be treated with respect.
- Herbal teas like Chamomile, Lemon Balm and Rooibos are great calmatives for babies aged 6 months and over, and their mothers too.
- Essential oils are excellent aids but, again, need to be used with care.
- Never ingest essential oils or place them neat on the skin.
- Keep them out of reach of your child.

In the next chapter you will learn a little more about the Cry It Out Approach and an alternative to it.

CHAPTER 4: THE CRY IT OUT APPROACH

"People who say they sleep like a baby usually don't have one." **Leo J. Burke**

In this chapter, you are going to learn about a very popular method for managing a crying baby – the Cry It Out Approach and an alternative approach that you can use if you want to.

Cry It Out Approach

The Cry It Out Approach is the more traditional approach. There are going to be times when your baby is crying just because they want attention or because they are bored. Proponents of this approach believe that, unless the baby has a physical need, like a diaper change or feeding, they should be left to cry until they tire themselves out.

It's aimed at teaching your child to soothe themselves and become more independent. It can be nerve-wracking initially, because you will want to go and pick the baby up and the baby won't self-soothe in the course of one night.

At some stage, the baby will learn to cry only when it has a physical need such as a wet diaper. How long this takes can vary from child to child.

This approach does get a lot of flak in the media and, if you do adopt it, you may come up against someone that has decided that it is wrong. As with all things related to YOUR child, you choose the method that you feel works best for you and your baby.

You are doing the best you can. You know your child best and you know what works and what doesn't.

An Alternative

Yet, you may feel uncomfortable with the Cry It Out Approach. Then I suggest you try the alternative approach. This one falls more under the approach of attachment parenting, and means responding to baby every time he cries. This could mean picking him up and rocking him back to sleep or just giving his tummy a rub.

The theory is that the more responsive you are to the child, the more he learns that he can rely on you. This approach is good for parents who cannot put up with the wailing, albeit temporary, that generally features in the first method.

Of course, this does mean that you can expect to get up more often. With the first method, your baby learns to self-soothe fairly quickly. It's not fun but it teaches them not to cry for just any old thing. Once they have learned that, you won't need to get up to check on them nearly as often.

Which Should I Choose?

No one can tell you which approach is correct. There are people on both sides of the debate who are convinced that their side is right. Whichever approach you use, you are bound to find someone telling you that you are wrong.

At the end of the day, it doesn't matter. Are they there to help you night after night while your baby is crying? You are the child's parents and you are the only people qualified to make that decision. And yes, you can change your mind if you find one approach is not working for you.

Being a parent involves a steep learning curve for all of us and no one has any right to judge you for how you choose to deal with this particular issue.

Do what is right for you and your child and you will both be happier for it in the long run.

To recap, in this chapter you have learned:

- The more traditional Cry It Out Approach means only responding to your baby's cries when they have a physical need. The idea behind the approach is that it teaches them to be more self-reliant. It is an approach that takes patience because it could take some time to work but it may reduce your workload further down the line.
- An alternative is where you attend to baby every time that they cry. The idea behind this approach is that they learn that they can always rely on you. You can expect to do more work with this approach.
- There is no one right or wrong answer here. This has been the subject of debate for many years and everyone has an opinion. The ONLY people who are qualified to make the decision about which approach to try are the child's parents. So you do what you feel is right and don't let anyone bully you or make you feel bad about your choice.

In the next chapter, you will learn that the first step in getting your baby to sleep through the night is to make sure that their sleep environment is safe and secure.

CHAPTER 5: MAKING YOUR BABY'S SLEEPING ENVIRONMENT A SAFE PLACE

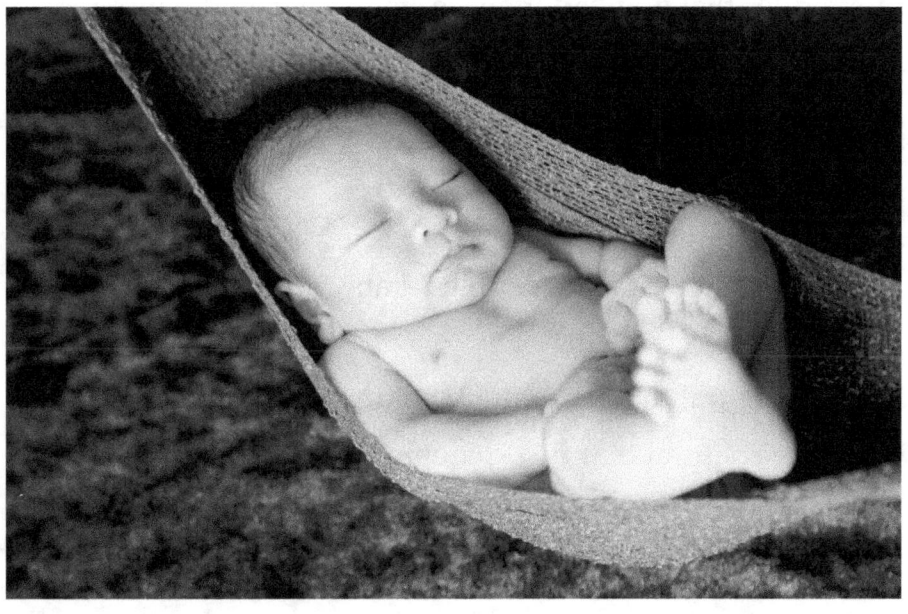

"When your child is driving you crazy, don't forget what you did to your parents." **Nana Nkrumah**

In this chapter, you will learn how to make sure that your baby's sleeping environment is as safe for them as possible.

Before baby arrives, we spend a lot of time making sure that our home is as safe as possible. We read the books, and we know all the helpful advice. We are going to do everything right.

Then baby arrives. We are still doing everything right. Fast-forward a couple of weeks of awful sleep, and suddenly the safety rules that you had in place start to get a little more flexible. Like when baby has finally fallen asleep on the sofa, and you don't want to wake them by moving them, you leave them there.

No harm in that, right? No, unless baby falls off.

It's only natural that parents are going to make mistakes. It's even more natural that tired parents will make mistakes. However, your baby's safety should always come first.

Sudden Infant Death Syndrome (SIDS)

SIDS is a syndrome that is most prevalent in babies aged between one month and four months. It can affect babies up to the age of a year old. What happens is simple. You put your baby down in their crib to sleep, and they never wake up.

It's devastating to deal with and, in many cases, it seems to happen without reason. There is no way of guaranteeing that your baby is safe – we don't know exactly what causes SIDS yet – but there are ways of reducing the risks.

- Teach your baby to sleep on their back rather than their stomach. The reason this is thought to help is that it is believed that it helps babies breathe more easily.
- Napping in a stroller, or something like that is fine. This is often comfier for baby and not harmful to them if the device is appropriately secure, and you are nearby. (You also don't have to risk waking your baby by moving them.)
- Check your baby periodically if they tend to sleep on their tummy. When they are sound asleep, you can consider turning them over.
- Make sure that you have a crib mattress that is firm, not lumpy, and that you use sheets that are taut on it.
- Remove toys and any other items from the crib. If the baby has one favorite toy, let them keep that.

- Keep the room temperature even and comfortable. Don't ratchet it up and let your baby overheat.
- Keep baby warm with the clothes that they wear, rather than relying on blankets.
- If the baby is sick, get them to the pediatrician or stay up with them all night.

Check The Crib For Comfort And Safety

Making sure that the baby is as comfortable as possible in their crib pays dividends for you as the parents. Here's what to look out for:

- Loose boards, or snaps that baby might pinch baby if they get caught in them.
- Your crib mattress must fit snugly in the crib. There should be less than an inch of space between the edge and the mattress. The more space there is, the higher the likelihood that baby will pinch themselves on it.
- Make sure that the crib sheets fit very well.
- Trim down the ends of any bumper ties.
- As soon as baby starts to stand, take out anything in the crib that it can use to climb out.

- Your crib should be stable. It is best to get as plain a crib on the inside as possible. Leave the decorative touches on the walls of the room. Babies can use those decorative flounces to climb out of bed.
- Always make sure that the side rail is securely locked into place.
- If you have a mobile for baby, make sure that they can see it but not stand up and reach it, or they might pull it down and hurt themselves.
- Check the specifications for the crib that you are using to ensure that it is the right one for your baby's age and weight.
- At night, you should be able to hear your baby. Either keep the crib close to the bed or use a good baby monitor. This will allow you to discern between the usual noises they make and when they are in distress.
- If you sleep with the baby in your bed, follow the same safety precautions in securing the bed. They should never be left on the open edge of the bed, and you should remove your bedding as well. You'll have to dress warmly just like the baby.

To recap, in this chapter, you have learned how to make your baby's sleeping environment safe and comfortable:

- Make sure that everything is as secure as possible.
- Bedding should fit well.
- The crib mattress should be flat and even.
- Reduce the number of things that might potentially get in the way of breathing.
- Back sleeping is the safest sleeping position for your baby.
- Reduce the number of ways that baby can use to climb out of the crib.

In the next chapter, you will learn more about how your baby sleeps and what is considered normal.

CHAPTER 6: HOW DOES YOUR BABY SLEEP?

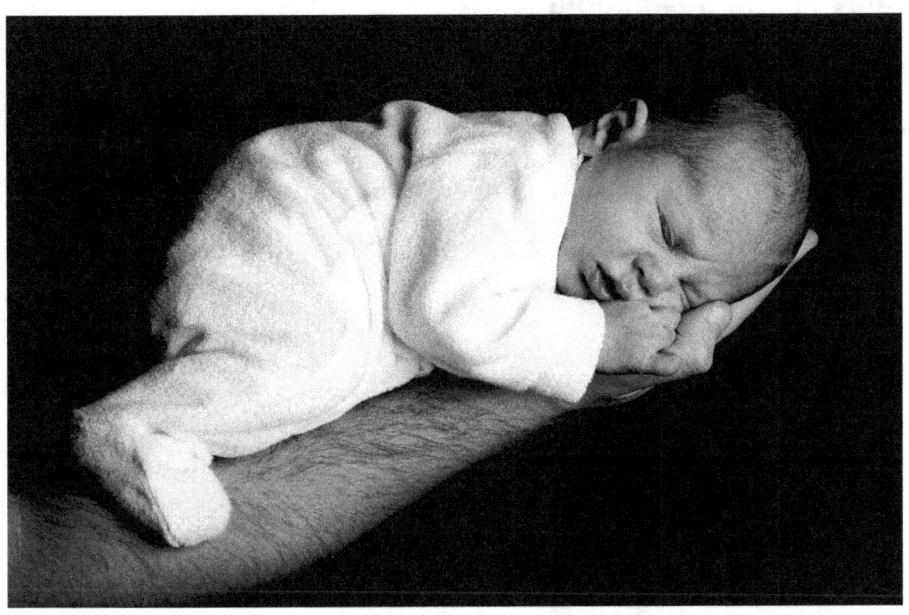

"Before I had my baby I could just get up and go whenever and wherever I wanted, sleep, eat and shower when I wanted...& now I can still do those things... Just after he eats, after he sleeps, after he gets a bath...it's crazy how much your life and your priorities change when you have a baby. It's not always easy but every moment is definitely worth it! I wouldn't change it for the world."
Kasi

The old chestnut "Sleep like a baby" is probably the first thing that comes to mind when we talk about baby sleep. However, the younger the baby is, the less soundly it is likely to sleep.

Baby Is Still Developing

Your baby is still developing. They don't have the same sleep / wake cycles we do. For starters, they need a lot more sleep than we do. They also need to have regular snacks – their tummies aren't as big as ours, so two or three meals is not enough to keep them going all day.

For the first few months of baby's life, his sleep cycle is still being set, so sleeping and waking is erratic. As baby ages, this starts to settle more and begins to correspond more to whether it is day or night.

The younger the baby, the more likely his sleep is light. This is part of a survival mechanism so that they are more aware of their environment and can respond to danger. The babies go through the same sleep cycles we do but cycle through them a lot faster. They also have brief periods where they are awake. (Again, a survival mechanism.)

So, it is normal for babies to wake up often. This makes it possible for them to assess whether they need anything, like a diaper change or food.

When Will My Baby Sleep Through The Night?

Remember how I was saying that babies have different sleeping cycles and need to snack often? Your version of sleeping through the night and your babies are entirely different. For a baby, four or five hours is the whole "night."

When can you expect that blissful four- or five-hour night to kick in? This will differ from baby to baby, but it usually is not before they are six months old at the very earliest.

It could be anytime between then and when they are two years old. As soon as your baby starts showing signs that they are ready to start sleeping for more extended periods of time, there are ways to help this process along. Once they are sleeping four or five hours at a stretch, you can work on stretching that out to a full seven or eight hours as well.

This was a short chapter. To recap, here's what you have learned:

- A baby's sleep cycles are erratic at first.
- They need to wake more often, at least initially.
- A "night" for your baby is not as long as a night for you.

In the next chapter, you will learn how you can start to set up a daytime routine.

CHAPTER 7: SETTING UP A DAYTIME ROUTINE

"The one advice that I would give just to moms who have a child or a newborn is definitely sleep while the baby sleeps. I've heard that so many times. I never realized how true it really is. If you don't, you'll be walking around like a zombie." **Tia Mowry**

In this chapter, you will learn how you can set up a routine that will help you get baby settled faster and sleeping for longer.

Observe Your Baby

Hopefully, you will never have had to go to a sleep clinic. If you did, though, do you know what the first thing the doctors would do to diagnose issues? Observe you sleeping. That's how they determine whether your sleep is disturbed.

You need to do the same for baby. You are going to keep a diary of how they sleep, where they sleep, what makes them sleepier and what makes them wider awake. You are going to need to watch them carefully for a few days so that you can see whether there is some pattern to their sleeping and waking.

I know that it seems like a tedious chore on a to-do list that is already overflowing, but this is an essential step in getting to the root of any issues. You'll use this information to set up a routine aimed at getting your baby off to sleep when you want them to.

Observe the following:

- **The environment**: Is it light, dark, quiet, or noisy?
- **The activity preceding sleep**: Is it calm, or active? Does baby seem to get overexcited and unable to sleep or does he just seem to run out of juice and collapse?
- **Where does baby like to sleep**? Do they fall asleep quickly in your arms, or in their stroller? This is likely where they feel the most secure, and it is usually going to be in your arms. That's not to say that they should stay in your arms throughout, but let them nod off there if they like. You can put them down when they are fast asleep.
- **Do they fall asleep when eating**? This is also reasonably natural behavior. Your baby's food need is met and, so, he falls asleep. The danger here is that they continue to suckle and associate suckling with sleep. They then start to need to suckle or suck on a pacifier to drift off. You can prevent this easily enough by watching your baby while they are suckling. When you can see they have had enough, take the bottle / breast away from them. If they get too fussy, you can always give it back but, over time, they will learn not to need this to fall asleep.

Record your daily observations in a diary. After 1-2 weeks, see if you can spot a pattern of things that seem to put baby asleep. Also take note anything that appears to have the opposite effect: a crying baby.

Some Helpful Tricks

Hopefully, you are reading this before you have brought baby home. I know that most people will, however, have turned to this book in a desperate quest to get a full night's sleep after the baby has been keeping them up all night. Try these tricks anyway and see if they work for you. If not, use them for the next baby.

If you have been watching your baby, you know when they start to look tired. Try putting them in their crib when you notice they are tired and see if they fall asleep. It often works with a younger child and is a fantastic way to get them to associate their cribs with sleep.

The next trick is to learn when you need to pick your baby up so that you can rock them to sleep, or when you can leave them to fall asleep on their own. This is where the work you did in observing your baby's habits is going to come in handy.

Not every noise that your baby makes at night means that they need attention. Sometimes it's just a natural noise that they make in their sleep. Like when your dog barks when it's dreaming, for example. If you pick them up every time you do this, you are disturbing their sleep and getting them into the habit of waking up more often.

By knowing what the different sounds mean, you can attend to your baby's needs as fast as possible so that, hopefully, they don't have time to wake up completely. That's where it is going to be useful to know what the baby's hungry cry is and what a typical sleeping sound is.

The next problem is that your baby sleeps a lot. A newborn can sleep as much as eighteen hours a day. This means that they are going to be sleeping during the day as well as during the night without really being able to distinguish the two.

Putting your baby to sleep in a quiet, dark room at midday may seem to be a good idea, but it does nothing to help your baby learn the difference between nighttime and daytime. I'm not saying that you should put them down in the middle of a football field during band practice, but, if they are sleeping during daylight, keep the blinds open, and consider playing soft music.

At nighttime, you can make it as quiet and as dark as possible to help them learn the difference between dark and light. When feeding the baby at night, keep things calm and collected. If you want to sing to them, do so very quietly. Get your nighttime routine as polished as possible by keeping everything that you need to feed the baby with nearby. Minimize the amount of time that baby is awake for.

Changing diapers is more of a challenge. You don't want your baby to lie in a dirty diaper for hours at a time, but you also don't want to go to the opposite extreme and change clean diapers because you think you should.

It's difficult not to wake baby when changing a diaper because of the logistics involved – you need to be able to see what you are doing and will be moving baby, cleaning them, etc. This is where disposable diapers that channel the moisture away from the baby's skin are very useful.

Again, get your routine down. Have everything that you need nearby and make sure that you have a small light that can allow you to see what you are doing without making things too bright.

Come Up With A Plan Of Action

Now that you have an idea of what makes your baby more wakeful and what makes them sleepier, you can start to come up with a plan of action that makes sense to you. This is where you are going to start setting up a routine for you and baby to follow.

The more ingrained the routine becomes, the easier it is to get baby asleep and to get baby to stay sleeping as well. Here we are going to go through what makes a good routine.

Daytime Should Also Have A Routine

The goal is to get your baby to learn the difference between day and night as fast as possible. Your nighttime routine is about signaling to them that it is time for bed.

Your early morning routine, when you want them up and about, is signaling that the day is starting. Make some clear distinction between just getting up from a nap and for a nighttime feed.

You could start, for example, introducing keywords. When you are getting your little one up and about, you could say, "Good morning, it's time to get up now." Keep that phrase for when you wake them for the day only. They will soon start to associate it with getting out of bed.

Next up, you could change them out of their pajamas and wipe down their faces. Again, this is a way of distinguishing day from night.

Get them ready to eat breakfast. You get the idea.

Monitor The Number Of Feeds During The Day

Some babies start to associate feeding with every time they wake up. When babies are small, they need food every few hours, as they begin getting older though, they can go a little longer without it.

Speak to your pediatrician about the right time to start implementing fewer night feeds and more day feeds. Your goal is to give them a full meal just before bedtime, but most of the rest of their food during the day. Your baby doesn't need as much energy when asleep, so should be eating more during the day anyway. It helps them sleep longer because they won't wake up as often due to hunger.

Monitor What They Eat

You also need to ensure that they are getting enough of the right sort of nutrients. Feeding them slow-release carbs and healthy foods that contain some fiber when they are ready will keep little tummies fuller for longer. If they have a slow release carb before bedtime, they will be able to sleep better because their blood sugar will be more balanced.

You also want to avoid foods that rev them up, especially close to bedtime. Sugary cereals may be delicious for them, but the sugar can give them too much energy before bedtime. This is never a good thing.

Daytime Naps

Establishing a routine when it comes to daytime naps is also going to help them sleep better at night. It might sound a bit contradictory, but good daytime napping enhances baby's sleep at night as well.

The key is to get napping right. Start to nudge them into a good routine by winding down activities when naptime is coming up. Naps should be at least an hour long to do baby any good but never more than three hours.

Limiting daytime naps is an excellent technique to ensure that your baby is tired enough to sleep at night. I understand that it is tempting to take advantage of this little break, but you are doing more harm than good by indulging the baby, and yourself, this way.

Gently nudge baby to get them to wake up and then try playing with them a little to get them to full alertness. It may sound cruel, but it really is one of the best ways to instill good sleeping habits.

The other side to this is, of course, not keeping baby awake for too long. A tired baby can be a cranky baby. An overtired baby can be a nightmare. If you start to learn the signs that baby is getting ready to sleep, you can put them to bed for a nap before they get over-tired.

Try to space out nap times evenly. If your baby naps three times a day, make these mid-morning, early afternoon, and early evening. If they only nap twice, leave out the evening nap, and, if they just nap once a day, make it in the afternoon.

Because you have been observing your child, you should now know what that signs are that they are tired. Usually, these include:

- ☐ Rubbing eyes
- ☐ Losing interest in playing
- ☐ Yawning
- ☐ Trying to lie down
- ☐ Eyes are glazing over
- ☐ Lowered levels of activity

Once your daytime routine is established, we can move onto your nighttime routine.

These are different ways in which you can set up a daytime routine. In this chapter, you have learned:

- That observing your baby's habits for a few days is the first step in getting your routine down.
- To prepare as much as possible before night feedings, etc. so that they go off without a hitch.
- That daytime naps are essential, regarding frequency and length.
- And that a good daytime routine is essential if you want to establish a good nighttime routine.

In the next and final chapter, you will learn about what a good nighttime routine consists of.

CHAPTER 8: YOUR NIGHTTIME ROUTINE

"I can't possibly take time off for a second baby, unless I do, in which case that is nobody's business and I'll never regret it for a moment unless it ruins my life." **Tina Fey**

In this last chapter, we will go through what constitutes a good nighttime routine and how you can prepare the way for sleep at night.

Again, you want to make it clear to the baby that this is not just an ordinary nap but bedtime.

A sample routine could be:

- ☐ Bathing baby and giving him a massage
- ☐ Reading him a story
- ☐ Singing him a calm song
- ☐ Playing soft, calming music
- ☐ Taking him for a walk
- ☐ Rocking him for a while
- ☐ Giving him his meal
- ☐ Say "Goodnight"

Two Hours Before Bedtime

Start dimming the lights and turn the TV down. Remove noisy toys and let baby play with more calming toys. Everything is geared towards slowing things down right now.

An Hour Before Bedtime

Move into the bedroom and sit with the lights as dim as you can manage. You should have just enough light to be able to read a book.

Everything slows down, and things fall into place. In the same order every night and, where possible, at around the same time. This preps baby for sleep - he knows that after you rock him, he has his food and then nods off. Over time, he will become drowsy at the right time.

When Is A Good Bedtime?

If you stay up later, you sleep more soundly and for longer, so that should work for baby as well, shouldn't it? Except that it won't. If you want to set yourself up for a disrupted night, a lot of crying and an overtired child, this is the way you start.

We were talking about the baby's sleep cycle earlier, remember? They are primed to fall asleep earlier in the evening. If left to their own devices, they would retire at 7:00 pm at the very latest.

While this may not be the most convenient time for you, working within this period will make it a lot easier to get your baby to bed without a screaming match. Yes, they will wake earlier, but they would have done that anyway.

Would you rather struggle for an hour to get them to sleep or save both of you the stress? Start bedtime procedures early on and let them be asleep by 7:00 pm at the very latest. Your baby will sleep better and be less cranky in the morning.

To recap, in this chapter you have learned:

- That a set nighttime routine is your best bet to get baby to sleep.
- Start preparing for bed at least two hours before bedtime.
- Babies need to go to sleep earlier than adults do.

FINAL WORDS

Well done, you made it to the end of the book! Believe me, when you are battling sleep deprivation and wrangling a cranky baby, that in itself is a big deal.

With this book, you have learned how to establish a set routine for your child, a routine that helps to minimize meltdowns. The more established the routine becomes, the more smoothly everything will work in future.

You have also learned some simple tips and tricks that will help you if your child does have a meltdown. And no matter how well-prepared you are, that will happen from time to time. The difference is that, now that you understand what's going on, these will be the exception rather than the rule.

Pat yourself on the back moms and dads – you have taken your first steps to be the parents everyone else envies. You will be the ones handing out the sage advice to the next set of sleep-deprived parents and telling them how easy it is. Just wait and see, you will get it right.

All the best of luck and love to you and your little one!

RESOURCES

Here are a few resources for suggested further reading, and some to just have a laugh!

Websites

- Happiest Baby on the Block – Harvey Karp
- www.babysleepsite.com
- www.babysleep.com
- violetsleepbabysleep.com
- www.mybabysleepguide.com
- www.isisonline.org.uk
- raisingchildren.net.au/sleep/babies_sleep.html
- goodnightsleepsite.com/baby-sleep
- newbiemom.com

Books

- Happiest Baby on the Block – Harvey Karp

- *The Sleepeasy Solution* – Jennifer Waldburger and Jill Spivack
- *Secrets of the Baby Whisperer* – Tracy Hogg and Melinda Blau
- How to Get Your Baby to Sleep without Being Held – Polly Moore
- *Go the F**k to Sleep* - Adam Mansbach. (I especially recommend the audiobook version, narrated by Samuel L. Jackson. Pulp Fiction meets Baby Sleep!)

For Fun

Go to Youtube, and watch these videos for some good laughs:

- Funny Baby Sleep - Funny Emotion Of Baby When Sleeping - So Fun, So Cute
- Baby won't go to sleep funny
- Baby won't go to sleep
- Baby stops crying when Father chants OM
- 12 Hilarious Comics That Nail The Reality Of Parenthood

DID YOU LIKE THIS BOOK?

If you enjoyed this book, I would like to ask you for a favor. Would you be kind enough to share your thoughts and post a review of this book? Just a few sentences would already be really helpful.

Your voice is important for this book to reach as many people as possible.

The more reviews this book gets, the more parents will be able to find it and enjoy more hours of sleep at night for both their baby and themselves.

Thank you again for reading this book and good luck with applying everything you have learned!

I'm rooting for you…

NOTES

www.ingramcontent.com/pod-product-compliance
Lightning Source LLC
Chambersburg PA
CBHW052116110526
44592CB00013B/1635